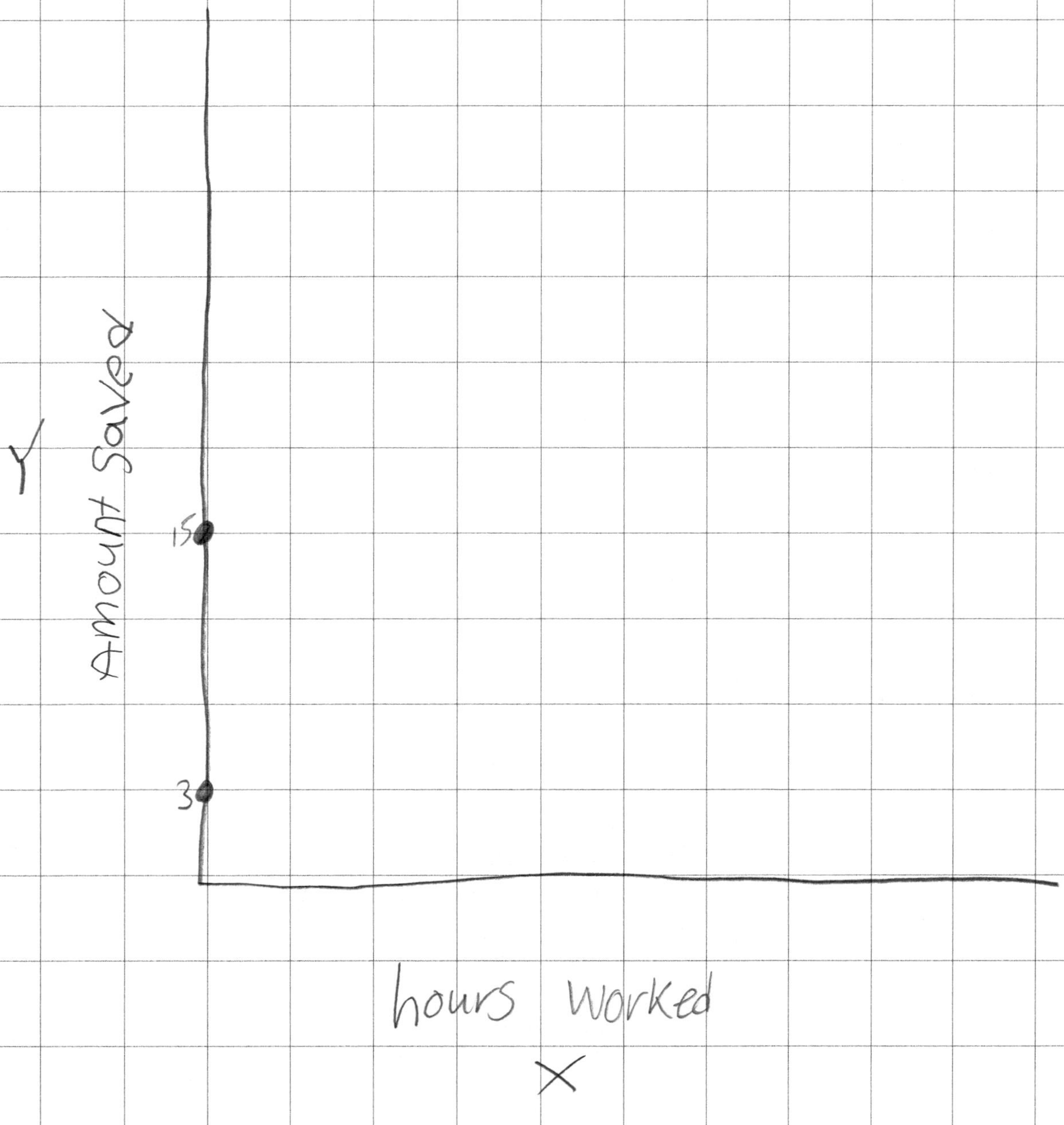

Y
Amount saved
15
3
hours worked
X

Made in the USA
Coppell, TX
05 February 2021

49661068R00063